THE BROONS

Diary 2015

Week-to-view Diary

Vital dates for 2015

Scottish Events and Historical Dates

Broons wisdom

Fun from the Happy Family that
makes every Family happy

BLACK & WHITE PUBLISHING

Important Information

This diary belongs tae:
_____

If Found, please return tae:
_____
_____
_____

Tel:
_____

In an emergency, please contact:
_____

Mobile:
_____

Home phone: _____ Work phone: _____

Email: _____ Work email: _____

Doctor: _____ Dentist: _____

Polis:
_____

Hair dresser:
_____

Bairns' school:
_____

Hoose insurance no: _____ Motor insurance no: _____

Life insurance no:
_____

Sweep: _____ Coal man: _____

Plumber: _____ Boolin' Club: _____

Day for the fish man: _____ Day for the rag man: _____

Bin day:
_____

Birthdays: _____ Appointments: _____
_____ _____
_____ _____

Anniversaries: _____ Celebrations: _____
_____ _____

THE BROONS

2015

JANUARY						
M	T	W	T	F	S	
			1	2	3	
5	6	7	8	9	10	
12	13	14	15	16	17	
19	20	21	22	23	24	
26	27	28	29	30	31	

FEBRUARY						
S	M	T	W	T	F	S
1	2	3	4	5	6	7
8	9	10	11	12	13	14
15	16	17	18	19	20	21
22	23	24	25	26	27	28

MARCH						
S	M	T	W	T	F	S
1	2	3	4	5	6	7
8	9	10	11	12	13	14
15	16	17	18	19	20	21
22	23	24	25	26	27	28
29	30	31				

APRIL						
S	M	T	W	T	F	S
			1	2	3	4
5	6	7	8	9	10	11
12	13	14	15	16	17	18
19	20	21	22	23	24	25
26	27	28	29	30		

MAY						
M	T	W	T	F	S	
				1	2	
4	5	6	7	8	9	
11	12	13	14	15	16	
18	19	20	21	22	23	
25	26	27	28	29	30	

JUNE						
S	M	T	W	T	F	S
	1	2	3	4	5	6
7	8	9	10	11	12	13
14	15	16	17	18	19	20
21	22	23	24	25	26	27
28	29	30				

JULY						
S	M	T	W	T	F	S
			1	2	3	4
5	6	7	8	9	10	11
12	13	14	15	16	17	18
19	20	21	22	23	24	25
26	27	28	29	30	31	

AUGUST						
S	M	T	W	T	F	S
						1
2	3	4	5	6	7	8
9	10	11	12	13	14	15
16	17	18	19	20	21	22
23	24	25	26	27	28	29
30	31					

SEPTEMBER						
M	T	W	T	F	S	
	1	2	3	4	5	
7	8	9	10	11	12	
14	15	16	17	18	19	
21	22	23	24	25	26	
28	29	30				

OCTOBER						
S	M	T	W	T	F	S
				1	2	3
4	5	6	7	8	9	10
11	12	13	14	15	16	17
18	19	20	21	22	23	24
25	26	27	28	29	30	31

NOVEMBER						
S	M	T	W	T	F	S
1	2	3	4	5	6	7
8	9	10	11	12	13	14
15	16	17	18	19	20	21
22	23	24	25	26	27	28
29	30					

DECEMBER						
S	M	T	W	T	F	S
		1	2	3	4	5
6	7	8	9	10	11	12
13	14	15	16	17	18	19
20	21	22	23	24	25	26
27	28	29	30	31		

Eleven Braw

To the tune of 'Three Blind Mice'.

Eleven braw Broons . . .
Eleven braw Broons . . .
  Did ever ye see such a family tree
For laughter – an' sometimes a tear in your e'e?
  They're a' true to life, for they're just YOU an' ME!
Eleven Braw Broons.

      Gran'paw's gettin' on . . .
      Gran'paw's gettin' on . . .
        He's the Broon that was in at the start.
      They may come mair handsome, but never as smart
        The secret, of course, is he's still young in heart.
      Gran'paw's gettin' on.

            Good old Hen and Joe . . .
            Good old Hen and Joe . . .
              They're both Paw Broon's sons,
            yet they're like chalk and cheese.
            It takes Joe a' his time to reach up
            to Hen's knees!
              It's left to the TWINS to be like as
            twa peas.
            Good old Hen and Joe.

Broons

Horace an' the Bairn . . .
Horace an' the Bairn . . .
  Most likely to go far of a' the crew.
One o' them has enough brains for two –
And butter wouldna melt in the other yin's mou'!
Horace an' the Bairn.

Bonnie Maggie Broon . . .
Bonnie Maggie Broon . . .
  She's as sweet as the rose clingin' to the wa'
An' she is the fairest o' them a' –
  "She gets it a' frae her feyther!" smirks Paw.
Bonnie Maggie Broon.

Daphne is a laugh . . .
Daphne is a laugh . . .
  She's looked for Romance forty years or mair,
An' never progressed past the foot o' the stair!
  But she "clicks" wi' us, so we shouldna care.
Daphne is the lass.

Then we come to Maw . . .
Then we come to Maw . . .
  If teethache strikes in the middle o' the night –
If judgement is needed to settle a fight –
  If a' this dreary old world needs put right –
THEN WE COME TO MAW!

Notable Dates

JANUARY
1st   New Year's Day (Ne'erday)
2nd   Bank Holiday (Scot, NZ)
14th   Makar Sankranti (Hindu Festival)
25th   Burns Night

FEBRUARY
14th   St Valentine's Day
17th   Shrove Tuesday
18th   Ash Wednesday, Lent begins

MARCH
1st   St David's Day (Wales)
6th   Holi (Hindu Festival)
15th   Mothering Sunday (UK, R of I, NI)
17th   St Patrick's Day (R of I, NI)
29th   Palm Sunday
29th   British Summer Time (BST) begins
      Irish Standard Time (IST) begins

APRIL
1st   April Fools Day, Huntigowk
2nd   Maundry Thursday
3rd   Passover begins (evening)
      Good Friday (except R of I)
4th   Easter Saturday, Lent ends
5th   Easter Sunday
6th   Easter Monday (except parts of Scotland)
11th   Passover ends
23d   St George's Day (England)

MAY
1st   Beltane
4th   Bank Holiday (UK, R of I)
10th   Mother's Day (Aus, Can, NZ, US)
18th   Victoria Day Public Holiday (Dundee, Edinburgh, Paisley, Livingston and Perth)
23rd   Shavuot (Jewish Holiday, begins in evening)
24th   Pentecost
25th   Spring Bank Holiday
31st   Trinity Sunday

JUNE
1st   Bank Holiday (R of I)
18th   Beginning of Ramadan
21st   Summer Solstice
21st   Father's Day (Can, R of I, UK, US)
      Midsummer E'en
24th   Midsummer Day
      St John the Baptist Day

JULY
4th   Trades Holiday (Edinburgh)
13th   Laylat al-Qadr (Muslim Night of Power)
15th   St Swithun's Day
18th   Glasgow Fair (Glasgow)
25th   Tisha B'Av begins (Jewish holiday, evening)
26th   Tisha B'Av ends (evening)

AUGUST
31st   Summer Bank Holiday (except Scotland)

SEPTEMBER
6th   Father's Day (Aus, NZ)
13th   Rosh Hashanah begins (Jewish New Year, evening)
15th   Rosh Hashanah ends (evening)
17th   Ganesh Chaturthi (Hindu Festival)
21st   Autumn Public Holiday (Edinburgh)
22nd   Yom Kippur begins (Jewish Festival, evening)
23rd   Yom Kippur ends (evening)
28th   Autumn Public Holiday (Glasgow)
29th   Michaelmas Day

OCTOBER
12th   Thanksgiving (Canada)
13th   Murharram begins (first month of Islamic calendar)
      Navaratri begins (Hindu Festival)
21st   Navaratri ends
22nd   Eid al-Adha (Muslim Festival, evening)
25th   British Summer Time (BST) ends
      Irish Standard Time (IST) ends
26th   Bank Holiday (R of I)
31st   Halloween, Samhain, Celtic New Year

NOVEMBER
1st   All Saints' Day
2nd   All Souls' Day
5th   Guy Fawkes' Night (UK)
8th   Remembrance Sunday
11th   Remembrance Day, Diwali (Hindu Festival)
12th   Murharram ends
29th   Advent Sunday
30th   St Andrew's Day (Scotland)

DECEMBER
6th   Hanukkah begins (evening)
14th   Hanukkah ends (evening)
22nd   Winter Solstice
24th   Christmas Eve
25th   Christmas Holiday
26th   Boxing Day
31st   New Year's Eve, Hogmanay (Scotland)

Festivals

JANUARY
1st   Kirkwall Ba' Game, Orkney
       The Loony Dook, South Queensferry
11th   Burning of the Clavie, Burghead, Moray
27th   Up Helly Aa, Lerwick, Shetland

FEBRUARY
17th   Fastern's E'en Ba', Duns
26th   Callant's Ba', Jedburgh

MARCH
1st   Whuppity Scoorie, Lanark

APRIL
30th   Beltane Fire Festival, Calton Hill, Edinburgh

MAY
11th   Gourock Highland Games, Inverclyde
23rd-24th Atholl & Breadalbane Gathering and Highland Games,
       Blair Castle
30th   British Piping Championship and West Lothian
       Highland Games, Bathgate Edinburgh

JUNE
5th-6th   Hawick Common-Riding, Hawick
6th   Shotts Highland Games, Shotts
7th-13th   Lanark Lanimers, Lanark
7th   Markinch Highland Games, John Dixon Park
12th   Selkirk Common Riding Day, The Borders
13th   *Bearsden and Milngavie Highland Games, Bearsden
       and Milngavie
14th   Ardrossan Highland Games, North Ayrshire
       Strathmore Highland Games, Glamis
       *Cupar Highland Games, Fife
16th   The Riding of the Marches, Linlithgow
19th-22nd Royal Highland Show, Edinburgh
20th   Lesmahagow Highland Games, Lesmahagow
       Oldmeldrum Sports and Highland Games, Oldmeldrum,
       Aberdeenshire
       Linlithgow & Linlithgow Bridge Children's Gala Day,
       Linlithgow
21st   * Newburgh Highland Games, North Fife
27th   *Drumtochty Highland Games, Drumtochty Glen
       Ceres Highland Games, Ceres

JULY
1st   *Kenmore Highland Games, Perthshire
4th   Aberdeen Highland Games, Aberdeen
       Glengarry Highland Games, Invergarry
       Luss Highland Games, Luss, Loch Lomond
       Annan Riding of the Marches, Annan, Dumfriesshire
10th-12th T in the Park, Strathallan Castle
10th   Jethart Callants Festival, Jedburgh
11th   Alva Highland Games, Alva
13th-19th IPC Swimming World Championships, Glasgow
18th   Locharron Highland Games, North West Highlands
       Inverness Highland Games, Highlands
       Tomintoul Highland Games, Aberdeen
18th   *Stonehaven Highland Games, Stonehaven

20th   *Burntisland Highland Games, Fife
21st   Inveraray Highland Games, Argyll and Bute
24th   Mull Highland Games, Argyll and Bute
24th   *Durness Highland Games
       Comrie Fortnight (until 8th August), Perthshire
       *Dufftown Highland Games, Moray
25th   Lochaber Highland Games, Fort William
25th-26th *Callander Highland Games, Stirling
25th   Strahconon Highland Games, Highlands
       Lochearnhead Highland Games, Loch Lomond
       Halkirk Highland Games, Highlands
31st   Langholm Common Riding, The Borders

AUGUST
1st   Lauder Common Riding, The Borders
       Aberlour Strathspey Highland Games, Aberlour, Moray
       Newtonmore Highland Games, Highlands
2nd   Bridge of Allan Highland Games, Stirling
5th   *Isle of Skye Highland Games, Portree, Isle of Skye
7th-29th   Royal Edinburgh Military Tattoo, Edinburgh
7th-31st   Edinburgh International Festival and Fringe, Edinburgh
8th   Abernethy Highland Games, Inverness
       Dundonald Highland Games, Ayrshire
       North Berwick Highland Games, East Lothian
9th   *Perth Highland Games, Perth
13th   Ballater Highland Games, Aberdeenshire
14th   Tain Highland Gathering, Highlands
15th-31st Edinburgh International Book Festival, Edinburgh
15th   Helmsdale and District Highland Games, Sutherland
       Rannoch Highland Gathering, Highlands
       Stirling Highland Games, Stirling
16th   Crieff Highland Gathering, Perth and Kinross
22nd   Glenfinnan Highland Games, Fort William
22nd   Lonach Highland Games, Aberdeenshire
       Bute Highland Games, Argyll and Bute
       Glenurquhart Highland Games, Drumnadrochit, Loch
       Ness
       Invergordon Highland Games, Invergordon, Highlands
       Strathardle Highland Games, Perthshire
23rd   Grantown on Spey Highland Games, Highlands
29th   *Birnam Highland Games, Perthshire
29th-6th   *Largs Viking Festival, Largs

SEPTEMBER
5th   Braemar Gathering, Aberdeenshire
       *Peebles Highland Games, The Borders
6th   Blairgowrie and Rattray Highland Games, Perthshire
12th   Pitlochry Highland Games, Perthshire
19th   *Invercharron Highland Games, Sutherland

OCTOBER
21st-25th *Dundee Literary Festival, Dundee
23rd-1st   November. World Gymnastic Championships, Glasgow

DECEMBER
25th   Kirkwall Ba' Game, Orkney
31st   Biggar's Bonfire, South Lanarkshire
       Comrie Flambeaux Procession, Perthshire
       Stonehaven Fireball Ceremony, Kincardineshire

Events marked thus * in the diary were still to be confirmed at the time of press and may be subject to change by the organisers. See individual websites for details.

WOMEN'S CLOTHING SIZE

UK	4	6	8	10	12	14	16	18	20	22	24
US	0	2	4	6	8	10	12	14	16	18	20
EU	34	36	38	40	42	44	46	48	50	52	54

GIRLS' DRESSES AND COATS

UK	3	5	7	9	11	13	15	17
US	1	3	5	7	9	11	13	15
EU	28	30	32	34	36	38	40	42

MEN'S SUITS, JUMPERS AND COATS

UK/US	38	40	42	44	46	48	50	52	54
EU	48	50	52	54	56	58	60	62	64

MEN'S SHIRTS

	S	M	L	XL	XXL	3XL	4XL
UK/US	14-14.5	15-15.5	16-16.5	17-17.5	18-18.5	19-19.5	20-20.5
EU	36	38-40	42-44	46-48	50-52	54-56	58-60

LADIES SHOES

UK	2	2.5	3	3.5	4	4.5	5	5.5	6	6.5	7	7.5	8
US	4.5	5	5.5	6	6.5	7	7.5	8	8.5	9	9.5	10	10.5
EU	34	35	35.5	36	37	37.5	38	38.5	39	39.5	40	41	42

MENS SHOES

UK	5	5.5	6	6.5	7	7.5	8	8.5	9	9.5	10	10.5	11	11.5	
US	5.5	6	6.5	7	7.5	8	8.5	9	9.5	10	10.5	11	11.5	12	12
EU	38	38.7	39.3	40	40.5	41	42	42.5	43	44	44.5	45	46	46.5	

Conversions

GIRLS SHOES

UK	8	8.5	9	9.5	10	10.5	11	11.5	12	12.5	13	13.5	1	1.5	2	2.5
US	8.5	9	9.5	10	10.5	11	11.5	12	13.5	1	1.5	2	2.5	3	3.5	4
EU	26	26.5	27	27.5	28	28.5	29	30	30.5	31	31.5	32.2	33	33.5	34	35

BOYS SHOES

UK	11	11.5	12	12.5	13	13.5	1	1.5	2	2.5	3	3.5	4	4.5
US	11.5	12	12.5	13	13.5	1	1.5	2	2.5	3	3.5	4	4.5	5
EU	29	29.7	30.5	31	31.5	33	33.5	34	34.7	35	35.5	36	37	37.5

HAT SIZES

UK	$6\frac{3}{8}$	$6\frac{1}{2}$	$6\frac{5}{8}$	$6\frac{3}{4}$	$6\frac{7}{8}$	7	$7\frac{1}{8}$	$7\frac{1}{4}$	$7\frac{3}{8}$	$7\frac{1}{2}$	$7\frac{5}{8}$
US	$6\frac{1}{2}$	$6\frac{5}{8}$	$6\frac{3}{4}$	$6\frac{7}{8}$	7	$7\frac{1}{8}$	$7\frac{1}{4}$	$7\frac{3}{8}$	$7\frac{1}{2}$	$7\frac{5}{8}$	$7\frac{3}{4}$
Inches	$20\frac{1}{2}$	$20\frac{7}{8}$	$21\frac{1}{4}$	$21\frac{5}{8}$	22	$22\frac{1}{2}$	$22\frac{7}{8}$	$23\frac{1}{4}$	$23\frac{5}{8}$	24	$24\frac{1}{2}$
Centimetres	52	53	54	55	56	57	58	59	60	61	62

THE BROONS' QUIET DAY

The Twins New Year Resolutions

Be nice tae Daphne.

Naw if she's wearin' yin o' her homemade dresses!

Dinnae steal cakes frae Maw.

Only lickin' the spoon is allowed.

Get as strong as Joe.

Aye! Then we can win at Fitba'

That's a' for now, we cannae think o' ony more!

Whit's your resolutions?

_____

_____

_____

_____

January

The year is starting anew but the celebrations continue. Ye cannae beat a guid haggis tae celebrate The Bard, Rabbie Burns, on the 25th o' January. So tak' up your glass o' whisky and mak' praise tae your haggis.

Address tae a Haggis

Fair fa' your honest, sonsie face,
Great chieftain o' the pudding-race!
Aboon them a' ye tak your place,
Painch, tripe, or thairm: Weel are ye wordy o'a grace
As lang's my arm.

The groaning trencher there ye fill,
Your hurdies like a distant hill,
Your pin wad help to mend a mill
In time o'need,
While thro' your pores the dews distil
Like amber bead.

His knife see rustic Labour dight,
An' cut you up wi' ready sleight,
Trenching your gushing entrails bright,
Like ony ditch;
And then, O what a glorious sight,
Warm-reekin', rich!

Then, horn for horn, they stretch an' strive:
Deil tak the hindmost! on they drive,
Till a' their weel-swall'd kytes belyve
Are bent like drums;
Then auld Guidman, maist like to rive,
Bethankit! hums.

Is there that owre his French ragout
Or olio that wad staw a sow,
Or fricassee wad make her spew
Wi' perfect sconner,
Looks down wi' sneering, scornfu' view
On sic a dinner?

Poor devil! see him owre his trash,
As feckless as wither'd rash,
His spindle shank, a guid whip-lash;
His nieve a nit;
Thro' bloody flood or field to dash,
O how unfit!

But mark the Rustic, haggis-fed,
The trembling earth resounds his tread.
Clap in his walie nieve a blade,
He'll mak it whissle;
An' legs an' arms, an' heads will sned,
Like taps o' thrissle.

Ye Pow'rs, wha mak mankind your care,
And dish them out their bill o' fare,
Auld Scotland wants nae skinking ware
That jaups in luggies;
But, if ye wish her gratefu' prayer
Gie her a haggis!

Rabbie Burns

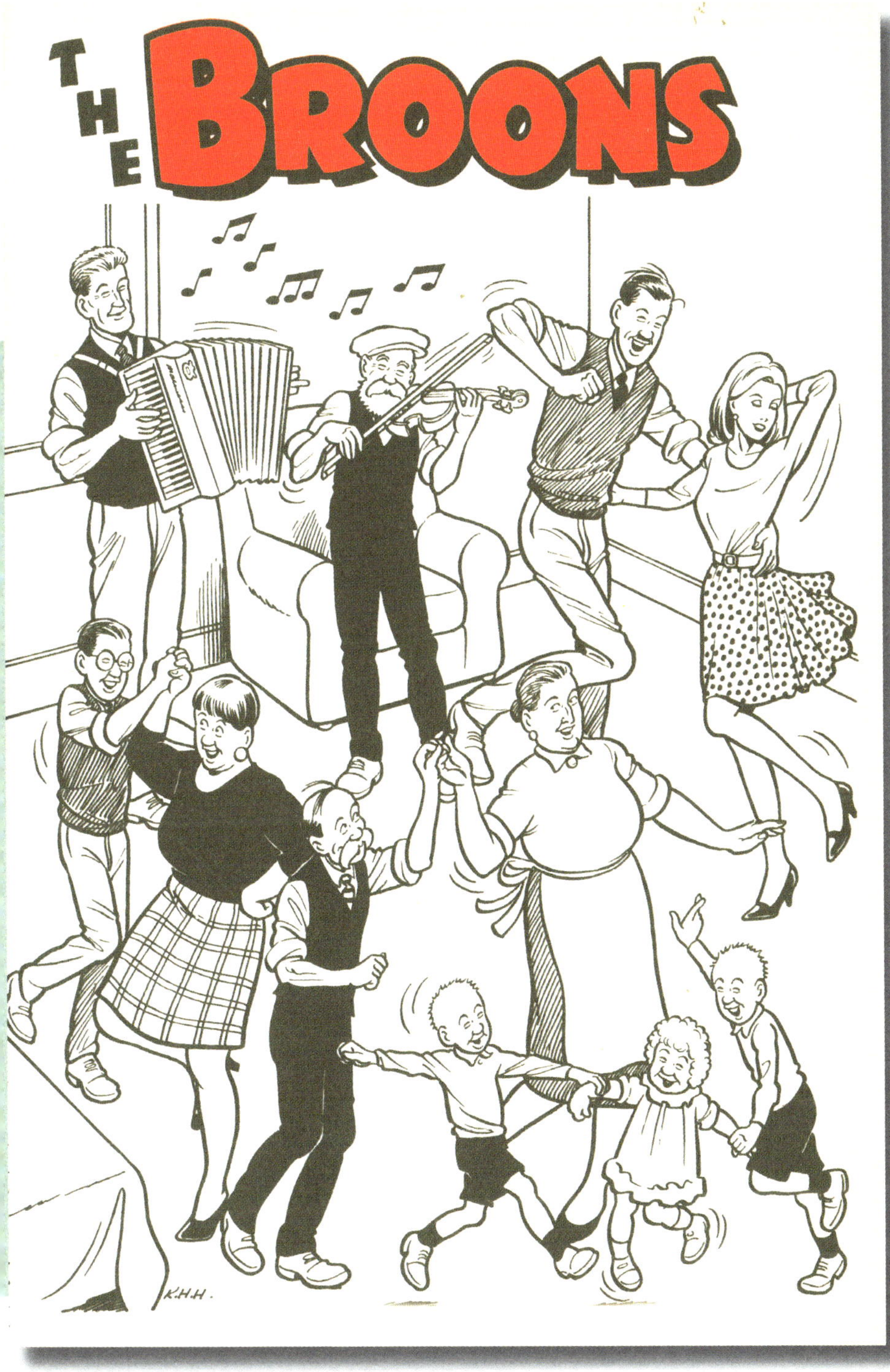
THE BROONS
K.H.H.

December 2014

29 Monday
_____
_____
_____
_____
_____
_____
_____
_____
_____
_____
_____
_____
_____
_____
_____
_____
_____
_____
_____
_____

30 Tuesday
_____
_____
_____
_____
_____
_____
_____
_____
_____
_____
_____
_____
_____
_____
_____
_____
_____
_____
_____
_____

31 Wednesday
Hogmanay
_____
_____
_____
_____
_____
_____
_____
_____
_____
_____
_____
_____
_____
_____
_____
_____
_____
_____
_____

January 2015

1 Thursday
New Year's Day, holiday

2 Friday
Holiday (Scot, NZ)

3 Saturday

4 Sunday

Wk	M	T	W	T	F	S	S
1				1	2	3	4
2	5	6	7	8	9	10	11
3	12	13	14	15	16	17	18
4	19	20	21	22	23	24	25
5	26	27	28	29	30	31	

January

5 Monday

Twelfth Night

6 Tuesday

Epiphany or Three Kings Day

7 Wednesday

January

8 Thursday

9 Friday

10 Saturday

11 Sunday

Wk	M	T	W	T	F	S	S
1				1	2	3	4
2	5	6	7	8	9	10	11
3	12	13	14	15	16	17	18
4	19	20	21	22	23	24	25
5	26	27	28	29	30	31	

January

12 Monday

13 Tuesday

14 Wednesday

Makar Sankranti, Hindu Festival

January

15 Thursday

_____
_____
_____
_____
_____
_____
_____
_____
_____
_____
_____
_____
_____
_____
_____
_____
_____
_____
_____
_____
_____
_____
_____
_____

16 Friday

_____
_____
_____
_____
_____
_____
_____
_____
_____
_____
_____
_____
_____
_____
_____
_____
_____
_____
_____
_____
_____
_____
_____
_____

17 Saturday

_____
_____
_____
_____
_____
_____
_____
_____
_____

18 Sunday

_____
_____
_____
_____
_____
_____
_____
_____
_____
_____
_____

Wk	M	T	W	T	F	S	S
1				1	2	3	4
2	5	6	7	8	9	10	11
3	12	13	14	15	16	17	18
4	19	20	21	22	23	24	25
5	26	27	28	29	30	31	

19 Monday

Holiday (NZ: Wellington)

Martin Luther King Jr. Day, holiday (US)

20 Tuesday

21 Wednesday

January

22 Thursday

_____
_____
_____
_____
_____
_____
_____
_____
_____
_____
_____
_____
_____
_____
_____
_____
_____
_____
_____
_____
_____
_____
_____

23 Friday

_____
_____
_____
_____
_____
_____
_____
_____
_____
_____
_____
_____
_____
_____
_____
_____
_____
_____
_____
_____
_____
_____
_____

24 Saturday

Vasant Panchami, Hindu Festival
_____
_____
_____
_____
_____
_____
_____
_____

25 Sunday

Burns Night
_____
_____
_____
_____
_____
_____
_____
_____
_____
_____

Wk	M	T	W	T	F	S	S
1				1	2	3	4
2	5	6	7	8	9	10	11
3	12	13	14	15	16	17	18
4	19	20	21	22	23	24	25
5	26	27	28	29	30	31	

January

26 Monday

Australia Day, holiday (Aus)

Holiday (NZ: Auckland)

27 Tuesday

Heritage Day (Can: YT)

28 Wednesday

January

29 Thursday

30 Friday

31 Saturday

1 Sunday

Wk	M	T	W	T	F	S	S
1				1	2	3	4
2	5	6	7	8	9	10	11
3	12	13	14	15	16	17	18
4	19	20	21	22	23	24	25
5	26	27	28	29	30	31	

February

Rabbie Burns always kens whit tae say.
Such a romantic!

My Luve is Like a Red, Red Rose

O my Luve's like a red, red rose,
That's newly sprung in June:
O my Luve's like the melodie,
That's sweetly play'd in tune.

As fair art thou, my bonie lass,
So deep in luve am I;
And I will luve thee still, my dear,
Till a' the seas gang dry.

Till a' the seas gang dry, my dear,
And the rocks melt wi' the sun;
And I will luve thee still, my dear,
While the sands o' life shall run.

And fare-thee-weel, my only Luve!
And fare-thee-weel, a while!
And I will come again, my Luve,
Tho' 'twere ten thousand mile!

Rabbie Burns

Yuck, romance is for lassies.
Do they no' ken that fitba' is
better for them?

THE TWINS

The Broons

CAR MANUAL
NOYUKI MKIII

February

2 Monday

Groundhog Day (Can, US)

Holiday (NZ: Nelson)

3 Tuesday

4 Wednesday

IT'S A'RIGHT, BAIRN. WE'RE COMIN', JIST A WEE DAB O' MAKE-UP . . .

I CANNAE DECIDE ABOOT THIS HAT.

WHIT? ABOOT WHETHER TAE BIN IT OR BURN IT? AN' IF THON'S A WEE DAB, I'D HATE TAE SEE A LOT.

February

5 Thursday

6 Friday

Waitangi day, holiday (NZ)

7 Saturday

8 Sunday

Wk	M	T	W	T	F	S	S
5							1
6	2	3	4	5	6	7	8
7	9	10	11	12	13	14	15
8	16	17	18	19	20	21	22
9	23	24	25	26	27	28	

February

9 Monday

Family Day, holiday (Can: AB, ON, SK)

Royal Hobart Regatta, holiday (Aus: TAS)

10 Tuesday

11 Wednesday

February

12 Thursday

13 Friday

14 Saturday

15 Sunday

Wk	M	T	W	T	F	S	S
5							1
6	2	3	4	5	6	7	8
7	9	10	11	12	13	14	15
8	16	17	18	19	20	21	22
9	23	24	25	26	27	28	

February

16 Monday

Washington's Birthday/Presidents' Day, holiday (US)

Holiday (Can: AB, ON, SK, MP, PEI)

17 Tuesday

Maha Shivaratri, Hindu festival

18 Wednesday

February

19 Thursday

Chinese New Year (Year of the Sheep)

20 Friday

21 Saturday

22 Sunday

Wk	M	T	W	T	F	S	S
5							1
6	2	3	4	5	6	7	8
7	9	10	11	12	13	14	15
8	16	17	18	19	20	21	22
9	23	24	25	26	27	28	

February

23 Monday

24 Tuesday

25 Wednesday

February / March

26 Thursday

27 Friday

Heritage Day (Can: YT)

28 Saturday

1 Sunday

St David's Day (Wales)

Wk	M	T	W	T	F	S	S
5							1
6	2	3	4	5	6	7	8
7	9	10	11	12	13	14	15
8	16	17	18	19	20	21	22
9	23	24	25	26	27	28	

March

Richt, enough o' a' this lazin' aboot. It's time tae get the hoose back in order, the new year has begun after a'! We dinnae want the neighbours thinkin' we dinnae tak' care o' oorselves noo, do we? Also, it's Mither's Day this month and ah want the place spotless!

Now, ah'm no here tae teach ye tae sook lemons, so here are a few wee cleaning tips for ye:

1. Tae pick up wee pieces o' glass, press a slice o' bread over the area, so you dinnae cut yer hand. Dinnae push too hard, mind, or the glass will go right through! Bread's also good for lifting blu-tac marks aff the walls.

2. If the flooers in your hoose are startin' tae look droopy, jist add a wee spoonful o' sugar in the watter tae brighten them up.

3. For stubborn stains on the bathtub, put on your usual cleaner but wipe it aff wi' half a grapefruit. The juice frae the grapefruit will lift the dirt gently and leave a nice smell in the bathroom.

4. Melted your shirt tae the iron? Nae bother – jist sprinkle salt on the ironing board and iron back and forth tae lift it.

5. Tae keep your scissors sharp, cut through a sheet of folded aluminium foil or a piece o' sandpaper.

6. If you're lucky enough tae have a microwave, ye can get rid o' ony bad smells by putting a cup o' watter in and microwave for five minutes, tae allow the watter tae steam. If it's a really stubborn smell, add a few drops o' lemon juice tae the watter first.

7. Your bairns have left pen marks on the table? Spray it wi' hairspray first and then wipe it clean aff.

8. If ye have jist finished cookin' a braw meal but the garlic smell has clung tae yer hands, gie them a wee rub against stainless steel (like your sink) before ye wash them with soap.

9. Tae lift stubborn pet hair frae the carpet that the hoover willnae lift, wheek yer hand into a clean trainer and brush it over the area. That'll lift it.

10. Ye really shouldn't be doing a' the cleaning alone. Get the faimily involved. Ye can mak' it a game for the bairns: set a timer – they need tae get the rug hoovered before the time runs oot.

THE BROONS

KEN·H·HARRISON.

March

2 Monday

3 Tuesday

4 Wednesday

March

5 Thursday

Purim, Jewish holiday (from sunset of 4th)

6 Friday

Holi, Hindu festival

7 Saturday

8 Sunday

Canadian Daylight Saving begins

Wk	M	T	W	T	F	S	S
9							1
10	2	3	4	5	6	7	8
11	9	10	11	12	13	14	15
12	16	17	18	19	20	21	22
13	23	24	25	26	27	28	29
14	30	31					

9 Monday

Commonwealth Day

Holiday (NZ: Taranaki. Aus: VIC, ACT, TAS, SA)

10 Tuesday

11 Wednesday

March

12 Thursday   **13** Friday   **14** Saturday

15 Sunday

Wk	M	T	W	T	F	S	S
9							1
10	2	3	4	5	6	7	8
11	9	10	11	12	13	14	15
12	16	17	18	19	20	21	22
13	23	24	25	26	27	28	29
14	30	31					

March

16 Monday

17 Tuesday

Shrove Tuesday

St Patrick's Day, holiday (R of I, NI)

18 Wednesday

Ash Wednesday, Lent begins

March

19 Thursday

20 Friday

21 Saturday

22 Sunday

Wk	M	T	W	T	F	S	S
9							1
10	2	3	4	5	6	7	8
11	9	10	11	12	13	14	15
12	16	17	18	19	20	21	22
13	23	24	25	26	27	28	29
14	30	31					

March

23 Monday

24 Tuesday

25 Wednesday

March

26 Thursday

_____
_____
_____
_____
_____
_____
_____
_____
_____
_____
_____
_____
_____
_____
_____
_____
_____
_____
_____
_____
_____
_____
_____
_____
_____
_____
_____
_____

27 Friday

_____
_____
_____
_____
_____
_____
_____
_____
_____
_____
_____
_____
_____
_____
_____
_____
_____
_____
_____
_____
_____
_____
_____
_____
_____
_____
_____
_____

28 Saturday

Rama Navami, Hindu festival
_____
_____
_____
_____
_____
_____
_____
_____
_____

29 Sunday

British Summer Time (BST) begins

Irish Standard Time (IST) begins

Palm Sunday
_____
_____
_____
_____
_____
_____

Wk	M	T	W	T	F	S	S
9							1
10	2	3	4	5	6	7	8
11	9	10	11	12	13	14	15
12	16	17	18	19	20	21	22
13	23	24	25	26	27	28	29
14	30	31					

April

How tae mak' the best egg for rolling doon hills:

1. Find the biggest egg in the box; elbow a' your brithers and sisters for it.
2. Get maw and paw tae help ye hard-boil the egg. It needs tae be hard-boiled 'cause if it's too soft, then it willnae last rolling doon the hill. If you are feelin' fancy, ask maw and paw tae put food colourin' in the watter first.
3. Once it's boiled, remove it frae the hot watter and let it cool. A game o' fitba' or tree climbin' is lang enough for the egg to cool, so ye dinnae burn your hands!
4. Now ye can get tae the guid bit – painting! Mak' sure ye have the brightest colours, so ye will be able tae see your egg at the bottom o' the hill.
5. Once you're a' finished painting and have tidied up, ye can get together wi' a' your pals and find the highest hill.
6. On the count o' three, all o' ye need to roll (or throw) your eggs doon the hill. Whoever's the last egg tae break wins! If you're feelin' brave, ye can even eat the egg!

THE BROONS

ANCIENT MONUMENT

SCOTLAND'S HAPPY FAMILY THAT MAKES EVERY FAMILY HAPPY

March / April

30 Monday

_____
_____
_____
_____
_____
_____
_____
_____
_____
_____
_____
_____
_____

31 Tuesday

_____
_____
_____
_____
_____
_____
_____
_____
_____
_____
_____
_____
_____
_____
_____
_____
_____

1 Wednesday

April Fool's Day

_____
_____
_____
_____
_____
_____
_____
_____
_____
_____
_____
_____
_____
_____
_____
_____

April

2 Thursday

3 Friday

Good Friday, holiday (except R of I)

4 Saturday

Holy Saturday, Lent ends

Hanuman Jayanti, Hindu festival

Passover begins (from sunset of 3rd)

5 Sunday

Easter Sunday

Daylight Saving Time ends (Aus: most locations, NZ)

Wk	M	T	W	T	F	S	S
9							1
10	2	3	4	5	6	7	8
11	9	10	11	12	13	14	15
12	16	17	18	19	20	21	22
13	23	24	25	26	27	28	29
14	30	31					

April

6   **Monday**

Easter Monday, holiday (except parts of Scot)

Tartan Day (Can, US)

7   **Tuesday**

Easter Tuesday, holiday (Aus: TAS, NZ: Southland)

8   **Wednesday**

April

9 Thursday

Vimy Ridge Day (Can)

10 Friday

11 Saturday

Passover ends

12 Sunday

Wk	M	T	W	T	F	S	S
14			1	2	3	4	5
15	6	7	8	9	10	11	12
16	13	14	15	16	17	18	19
17	20	21	22	23	24	25	26
18	27	28	29	30			

April

13 Monday

14 Tuesday

15 Wednesday

I BROCHT YE A BAG O' MIXED SWEETIES – I KEN THEY'RE YOUR FAVOURITES!

WHEN ME GROWS UP ME WANTS TAE BE JUST LIKE GRANPAW BROON, STILL WI' A SWEET TOOTH – BUT MEBBE WITHOOT THE WHISKERS!

#

16 Thursday

Emancipation Day, holiday (US, Washington DC only)

17 Friday

18 Saturday

19 Sunday

Wk	M	T	W	T	F	S	S
14			1	2	3	4	5
15	6	7	8	9	10	11	12
16	13	14	15	16	17	18	19
17	20	21	22	23	24	25	26
18	27	28	29	30			

20 Monday

21 Tuesday

22 Wednesday

April

23 Thursday

St George's Day (England)

24 Friday

25 Saturday

Anzac Day, holiday (Aus, NZ)

26 Sunday

Wk	M	T	W	T	F	S	S
14		1	2	3	4	5
15	6	7	8	9	10	11	12
16	13	14	15	16	17	18	19
17	20	21	22	23	24	25	26
18	27	28	29	30			

April

27 Monday

28 Tuesday

29 Wednesday

April / May

30 Thursday

1 Friday

2 Saturday

3 Sunday

Wk	M	T	W	T	F	S	S
14			1	2	3	4	5
15	6	7	8	9	10	11	12
16	13	14	15	16	17	18	19
17	20	21	22	23	24	25	26
18	27	28	29	30			

May

The days are gettin' warmer and the birds are startin' tae sing. Keep them singin' and harmonious wi' these feedin' tips for yer gairden:

Tips:

Birds aren't the only animals that would like tae eat the food ye put oot, so:

- Dinnae put food on the ground or low doon. It will attract mice and rats. Mak' sure any food dropped aff the table is cleared up.
- Place the table in a position that cats cannae jump ontae it. Avoid placing the table close tae bushes unless it's a holly bush or anither prickly plant.
- Grey squirrels are great climbers and the biggest challenge when you're tryin' tae prevent them frae gettin' up tae the table. Place a baffle around the stake tae stop the squirrels climbin'.

Whit tae feed the birds:

- Seed mixes. There are lots of bird seed mixtures available. Avoid mixes that contain split peas, beans or dried rice as only muckle birds will eat them.
- Fat balls. These are braw for the winter. Ye can buy them or make them: pour melted suet or lard ontae a mixture o' seeds, nuts, oatmeal, cheese or cake. Mak' it one-third fat, two-thirds mixture. Mix well and leave tae set in a container o' yer choice.
- Live mealworms are popular wi' robins and bluetits. Ye can buy them or rear them yourself (best speak tae the RSPC first and they can advise ye on how tae do it).
- Dinnae put oot milk, margarine, vegetable oils, dessicated coconut, cooked porridge oats, dry biscuits or mouldy and stale food.

4   Monday

Bank Holiday (UK, R of I)

Holiday (Aus: NT)

5   Tuesday

6   Wednesday

May

7 Thursday

8 Friday

9 Saturday

10 Sunday

Mother's Day (Aus, Can, NZ, US)

Wk	M	T	W	T	F	S	S
18					1	2	3
19	4	5	6	7	8	9	10
20	11	12	13	14	15	16	17
21	18	19	20	21	22	23	24
22	25	26	27	28	29	30	31

May

11 Monday

12 Tuesday

13 Wednesday

May

14 Thursday
Ascension Day

15 Friday

16 Saturday

17 Sunday

Wk	M	T	W	T	F	S	S
18					1	2	3
19	4	5	6	7	8	9	10
20	11	12	13	14	15	16	17
21	18	19	20	21	22	23	24
22	25	26	27	28	29	30	31

May

18 Monday

National Patriots' Day, holiday (Can: QC0)

Victoria Day, holiday (Scot: Edinburgh. Can: except QC)

19 Tuesday

20 Wednesday

May

21 Thursday

22 Friday

23 Saturday

24 Sunday

Shavot, Jewish holiday (from sunset of 23rd)

Whit Sunday or Pentecost

Wk	M	T	W	T	F	S	S
18					1	2	3
19	4	5	6	7	8	9	10
20	11	12	13	14	15	16	17
21	18	19	20	21	22	23	24
22	25	26	27	28	29	30	31

May

25 Monday

Memorial Day, holiday (US)

Spring Bank Holiday (UK)

26 Tuesday

National Day of Healing (Aus)

27 Wednesday

May

28 Thursday

29 Friday

30 Saturday

31 Sunday

Trinity Sunday

Wk	M	T	W	T	F	S	S
18					1	2	3
19	4	5	6	7	8	9	10
20	11	12	13	14	15	16	17
21	18	19	20	21	22	23	24
22	25	26	27	28	29	30	31

June

Ach, school's oot for the summer and I wis jist gettin' intae a' my studyin'. None o' mah brithers and sisters like tae study as much as I do. I always try tae have a wee project on the go for when I cannae get tae the library or when I'm feeling creative. This year, I'm tryin' tae be conscious o' the environment and try tae recycle a' mah old juice bottles and that got me thinkin': why don't I make Granpaw a hangin' gairden for a' his herbs oot o' plastic bottles? Braw idea, if I do say so mysel'! Means he won't have tae always trek tae his allotment.

Horace's Hangin' Herb Gairden
So, mak' sure you save a' o' your plastic bottles for this, or ye could mibbe use some old margarine tubs instead. I used three bottles 'cause Granpaw only has a small gairden at his hoose.

In two o' the three bottles, pierce four holes intae the sides. Two on the top and two on the bottom. On the third bottle, only pierce two on the same side. This one is gonnae be the bottom 'shelf' o' the gairden. It's no' got a hole on the bottom, so no watter drips through.

In a' o' the bottles, cut oot a rectangle on the side, between the two holes, so the bottle looks like a trough, ready tae be filled wi' soil and herbs.

This is where it gets a wee bit fiddly – you're aboot tae build the gairden! Lie aw o' the bottles on their side in a row and wi' a bit o' string or flexible wire, you're gonnae thread the string through a' the holes. Start wi' the bottom bottle (wi' only two holes) and tie a knot inside the bottle tae hold it a' together, then tie another knot in the string, tae hold the next bottle up and away from the bottom one, so it doesnae slip doon and crush the herbs. Continue ontae the next bottle and repeat the process on the other side. Once you have got a' the bottle tied together, tie the two bits o' string together, so ye can hang the bottle.

Find a nail or a ledge on a wall, so ye can hang the bottles up and then fill each one wi' soil or compost. Once you've done that, ye can plant your seeds!

When watering, pour watter intae the top bottle first, so a' the watter drips doon through the bottles.

The BROONS

Scotland's Happy Family That Makes Every Family Happy!

June

1 Monday

Bank Holiday (R of I)

Holiday (Aus: WA. NZ)

2 Tuesday

3 Wednesday

June

4 Thursday

Corpus Christi

5 Friday

6 Saturday

7 Sunday

Wk	M	T	W	T	F	S	S
23	1	2	3	4	5	6	7
24	8	9	10	11	12	13	14
25	15	16	17	18	19	20	21
26	22	23	24	25	26	27	28
27	29	30					

June

8   Monday

Queen's Birthday, holiday (Aus: except WA)

9   Tuesday

10   Wednesday

June

11 Thursday

12 Friday

13 Saturday

14 Sunday

Wk	M	T	W	T	F	S	S
23	1	2	3	4	5	6	7
24	8	9	10	11	12	13	14
25	15	16	17	18	19	20	21
26	22	23	24	25	26	27	28
27	29	30					

June

15 Monday

16 Tuesday

17 Wednesday

June

18 Thursday

Ramadan begins, Muslim observance (from sunset of 17th)

19 Friday

20 Saturday

21 Sunday

Father's Day (Can, R of I, UK, US)

Summer Solstice

Wk	M	T	W	T	F	S	S
23	1	2	3	4	5	6	7
24	8	9	10	11	12	13	14
25	15	16	17	18	19	20	21
26	22	23	24	25	26	27	28
27	29	30					

June

22 Monday

Discovery Day (Can: NFL)

23 Tuesday

24 Wednesday

St John the Baptist Day

La Fête Nationale du Québec (Can: QC)

June

25 Thursday

26 Friday

27 Saturday

28 Sunday

Wk	M	T	W	T	F	S	S
23	1	2	3	4	5	6	7
24	8	9	10	11	12	13	14
25	15	16	17	18	19	20	21
26	22	23	24	25	26	27	28
27	29	30					

July

"It's braw and the perfect drink for a picnic wi' freends and faimily. For the best picnic, dinnae forget a blanket, napkins, plastic bag for rubbish and some cups. I always forget the cups! "

The weather is warm and the days are still lang. How aboot this easy homemade lemonade tae enjoy wi' your picnic?

You will need:

A 2-litre/3½ pints pitcher

4 lemons, juiced
1 litre/1¾ pints of watter
100g/4oz caster sugar

Combine a' o' the ingredients together and stir until the sugar is dissolved. Chill in the refrigerator until ready tae drink.

June / July

29 Monday

30 Tuesday

1 Wednesday

Canada Day, holiday (Can)

Memorial Day (Can: NFL)

July

2 Thursday

3 Friday

4 Saturday

Independence Day, holiday (US)

5 Sunday

Wk	M	T	W	T	F	S	S
27			1	2	3	4	5
28	6	7	8	9	10	11	12
29	13	14	15	16	17	18	19
30	20	21	22	23	24	25	26
31	27	28	29	30	31		

July

6 Monday

7 Tuesday

8 Wednesday

July

9 Thursday

Nunavut Day (Can: NU)

10 Friday

11 Saturday

12 Sunday

Wk	M	T	W	T	F	S	S
27			1	2	3	4	5
28	6	7	8	9	10	11	12
29	13	14	15	16	17	18	19
30	20	21	22	23	24	25	26
31	27	28	29	30	31		

July

13 Monday

Battle of the Boyne, holiday (NI)

Laylat al-Qadr (Muslim Night of Power)

14 Tuesday

15 Wednesday

St Swithun's Day

THEY'RE JIST HAEIN' A WEE DANCE — NAE WILDER THAN THE HIGHLAND FLING!

July

16 Thursday

17 Friday

Eid al-Fitr (Ramadan ends)

18 Saturday

19 Sunday

Wk	M	T	W	T	F	S	S
27			1	2	3	4	5
28	6	7	8	9	10	11	12
29	13	14	15	16	17	18	19
30	20	21	22	23	24	25	26
31	27	28	29	30	31		

July

20 Monday

21 Tuesday

22 Wednesday

July

23 Thursday

24 Friday

25 Saturday

26 Sunday

Tisha B'Av, Jewish holiday (from sunset of 25th)

Wk	M	T	W	T	F	S	S
27			1	2	3	4	5
28	6	7	8	9	10	11	12
29	13	14	15	16	17	18	19
30	20	21	22	23	24	25	26
31	27	28	29	30	31		

July

27 Monday

28 Tuesday

29 Wednesday

July / August

30 Thursday

31 Friday

Summer Bank Holiday (UK, except Scot)

1 Saturday

2 Sunday

Wk	M	T	W	T	F	S	S
27			1	2	3	4	5
28	6	7	8	9	10	11	12
29	13	14	15	16	17	18	19
30	20	21	22	23	24	25	26
31	27	28	29	30	31		

August

The summer is nearly over but the Heilan' Games are aboot tae begin! The Hielan' Games isnae jist aboot athletic stuff. Great fun for a' the faimily.

There's loads o' kilties playin' bagpipes, drummers drummin' and dancers daein' the hielan' fling, fiddlers fiddlin' and strong men tossin' cabers the size o' telegraph poles. There's hammer throwers an' shot puttin' (like on the porridge box ye see at breakfast time).

In olden times, the chiefs o' a' the clans would mak' their men dae feats o' strength tae prove themselves as bonnie fechters.

The Tug-o'-War is a family favourite. Ye need a long thick rope wi' a centre mark and a mark at the head o' each team, and a mark on the ground. When the call comes tae 'HEAVE!', each team tries tae pull the other over the centre line.

There's even Scottish Heilan games a' over the world!

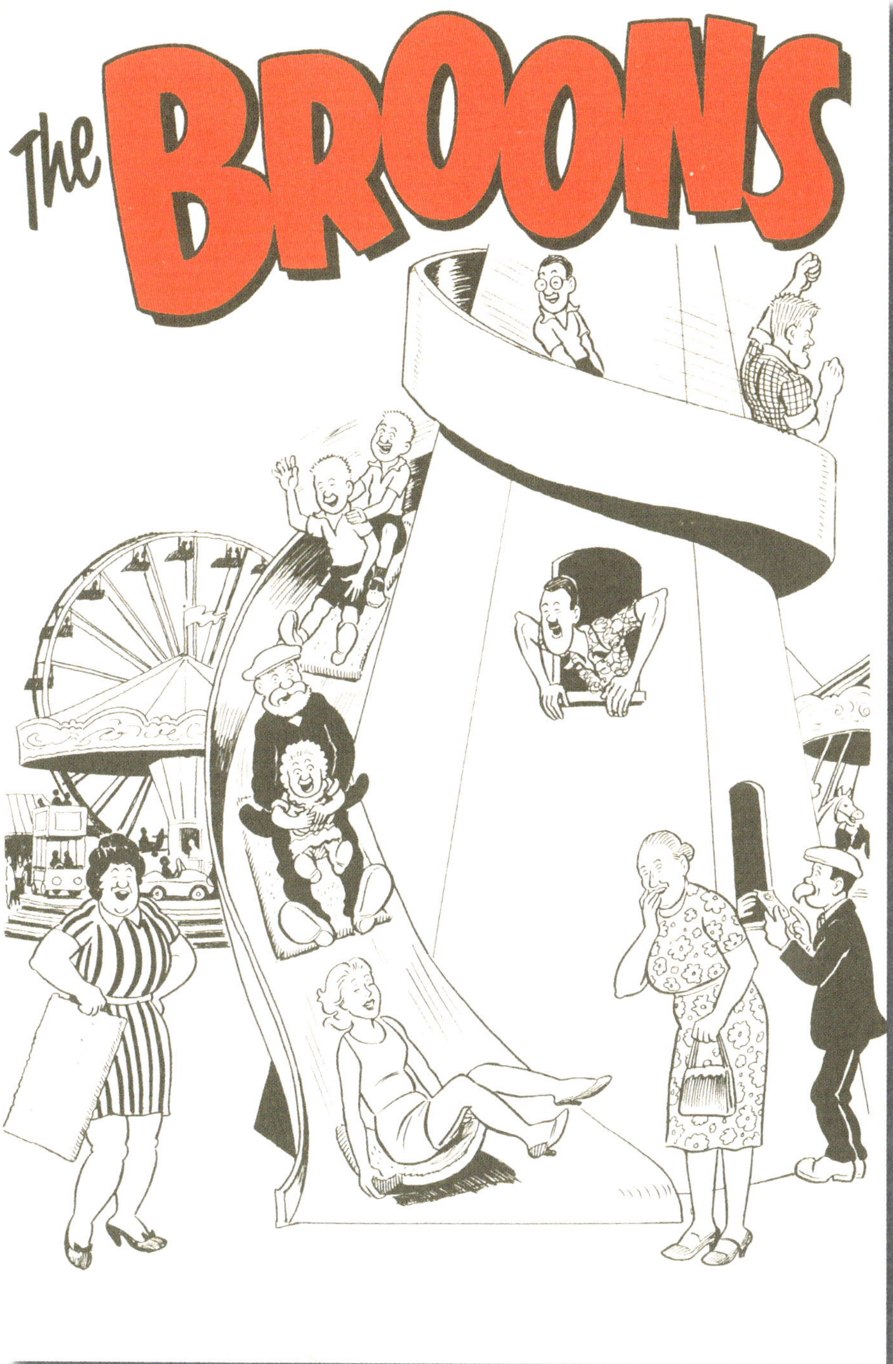
The BROONS

August

3 Monday

Summer Bank Holiday (Scot, R of I)

Holiday (Can: most areas. Aus: NT)

4 Tuesday

5 Wednesday

August

6 Thursday

7 Friday

8 Saturday

9 Sunday

Wk	M	T	W	T	F	S	S
31						1	2
32	3	4	5	6	7	8	9
33	10	11	12	13	14	15	16
34	17	18	19	20	21	22	23
35	24	25	26	27	28	29	30
36	31						

10 Monday

11 Tuesday

12 Wednesday

August

13 Thursday

14 Friday

15 Saturday

16 Sunday

Wk	M	T	W	T	F	S	S
31						1	2
32	3	4	5	6	7	8	9
33	10	11	12	13	14	15	16
34	17	18	19	20	21	22	23
35	24	25	26	27	28	29	30
36	31						

August

17 Monday

Discover Day, holiday (Can: YT)

18 Tuesday

19 Wednesday

August

20 Thursday

21 Friday

Gold Cup Parade (Can: PEI)

22 Saturday

23 Sunday

Wk	M	T	W	T	F	S	S
31						1	2
32	3	4	5	6	7	8	9
33	10	11	12	13	14	15	16
34	17	18	19	20	21	22	23
35	24	25	26	27	28	29	30
36	31						

24 Monday

25 Tuesday

26 Wednesday

August

27 Thursday

28 Friday

29 Saturday

30 Sunday

Wk	M	T	W	T	F	S	S
31						1	2
32	3	4	5	6	7	8	9
33	10	11	12	13	14	15	16
34	17	18	19	20	21	22	23
35	24	25	26	27	28	29	30
36	31						

September

The Autumn leaves are blowin' in and the scarves are comin' oot the drawers tae shield ye frae the cool wind. A' the bairns are back tae school and Winter is jist aroond the corner. It's a guid time o' year tae eat comfort food and sit by the fire in the evening.

Autumn Fires

In the other gardens
And all up the vale,
From the autumn bonfires
See the smoke trail!

Pleasant summer over
And all the summer flowers,
The red fire blazes,
The grey smoke towers.

Sing a song of seasons!
Something bright in all!
Flowers in the summer,
Fires in the fall!

Robert Louis Stevenson

THE BROONS

Scotland's Happy Family That Makes Every Family Happy

August / September

31 Monday   **1** Tuesday   **2** Wednesday

September

3 Thursday

_____
_____
_____
_____
_____
_____
_____
_____
_____
_____
_____
_____
_____
_____
_____
_____
_____
_____
_____
_____
_____
_____
_____
_____
_____
_____

4 Friday

_____
_____
_____
_____
_____
_____
_____
_____
_____
_____
_____
_____
_____
_____
_____
_____
_____
_____
_____
_____
_____
_____
_____
_____
_____
_____

5 Saturday

Krishna Janmashtami, Hindu festival

_____
_____
_____
_____
_____
_____
_____
_____

6 Sunday

Father's Day (Aus, NZ)

_____
_____
_____
_____
_____
_____
_____
_____
_____
_____

Wk	M	T	W	T	F	S	S
36		1	2	3	4	5	6
37	7	8	9	10	11	12	13
38	14	15	16	17	18	19	20
39	21	22	23	24	25	26	27
40	28	29	30				

September

7 Monday

Labor/Labour Day, holiday (US, Can)

8 Tuesday

9 Wednesday

September

10 Thursday

11 Friday

12 Saturday

13 Sunday

Wk	M	T	W	T	F	S	S
36		1	2	3	4	5	6
37	7	8	9	10	11	12	13
38	14	15	16	17	18	19	20
39	21	22	23	24	25	26	27
40	28	29	30				

September

14 Monday

Rosh Hashanah, Jewish New Year, begins

(from sunset of 13th)

15 Tuesday

Rosh Hashanah ends

16 Wednesday

September

17 Thursday

Ganesg Chaturthi, Hindu festival

18 Friday

19 Saturday

20 Sunday

Wk	M	T	W	T	F	S	S
36		1	2	3	4	5	6
37	7	8	9	10	11	12	13
38	14	15	16	17	18	19	20
39	21	22	23	24	25	26	27
40	28	29	30				

September

21 Monday

International Day of Peace (United Nations)

22 Tuesday

23 Wednesday

Eid al-Adha, Muslim festival of Sacrifice (from sunset of 22nd)
Yom Kippur, Jewish Day of Atonement (from sunset of 22nd)

September

24 Thursday

25 Friday

26 Saturday

27 Sunday

New Zealand's Daylight Saving Time begins

Wk	M	T	W	T	F	S	S
36		1	2	3	4	5	6
37	7	8	9	10	11	12	13
38	14	15	16	17	18	19	20
39	21	22	23	24	25	26	27
40	28	29	30				

September

28 Monday

Holiday (NZ: Canterbury [South]. Aus: ACT, WA)

First day of Sukkot, Jewish holiday (from sunset 27th)

29 Tuesday

30 Wednesday

October

1 Thursday

2 Friday

3 Saturday

4 Sunday

Last day of Sukkot, Jewish holiday

Australian Daylight Saving Time begins (most locations)

Wk	M	T	W	T	F	S	S
40				1	2	3	4
41	5	6	7	8	9	10	11
42	12	13	14	15	16	17	18
43	19	20	21	22	23	24	25
44	26	27	28	29	30	31	

October

Hallowe'en is braw for a' the faimily tae play and dress up. Ye get tae mak' silly faces oot o' pumpkins, dook for aipples and even mak' toffee aipples. Oor Maw Broon, she kens how tae mak' the best toffee aipples in a' o' Scotland.

TOFFEE AIPPLES

Aw ye got tae do is put 8 o' your favourite aipples into a bowl and cover wi' boiling watter tae remove the waxy coatin' o' the aipple. Then ye jist dry them wi' a towel, remove the stalk and put a lollypop stick in it.

Lay oot some baking parchment and put it near tae the stove. Pop the aipples on there. After ye've done that, put 100ml o' watter intae a pan and dissolve 400g o' golden caster sugar over a medium heat. Then stir in a teaspoon o' vinegar and four tablespoons o' golden syrup. Tak' a glass o' cold watter and put a few wee drips o' the sugar mix intae it. If it hardens instantly when it touches the watter, it's ready.

Noo tak' each aipple, and dip and twist them intae the hot toffee, letting any excess drip away. Then place them back ontae the baking parchment tae harden.

Once cool, hand them oot tae the bairns tae enjoy (jist watch ye dinnae crack a fillin' if ye try one).

Aye, we love tae mak' these in advance o' Hallowe'en, aboot twa days, so we can focus on getting dressed up for guisin'. It's always a shame though, withoot even tryin', Daphne always wins the fancy dress.

October

5 Monday
Labour Day, holiday (Aus: ACT, NSW, QLD, SA)

6 Tuesday

7 Wednesday

October

8 Thursday

9 Friday

Royal National Mod begins, Oban

10 Saturday

World Porridge Day

11 Sunday

Wk	M	T	W	T	F	S	S
40			1	2	3	4	
41	5	6	7	8	9	10	11
42	12	13	14	15	16	17	18
43	19	20	21	22	23	24	25
44	26	27	28	29	30	31	

October

12 Monday

Columbus Day, holiday (US)

Thanksgiving Day, holiday (Can)

13 Tuesday

Navratri begins, Hindu festival

14 Wednesday

Muharram, first month of the Islamic calendar, begins (from sunset of 13th)

October

15 Thursday

16 Friday

17 Saturday

Royal National Mod ends

18 Sunday

Wk	M	T	W	T	F	S	S
40				1	2	3	4
41	5	6	7	8	9	10	11
42	12	13	14	15	16	17	18
43	19	20	21	22	23	24	25
44	26	27	28	29	30	31	

October

19 Monday

20 Tuesday

21 Wednesday

Navratri ends

October

22 Thursday

23 Friday

Holiday (NZ: Hawke's Bay)

24 Saturday

25 Sunday

British Summer Time ends

Irish Winter Time begins

Wk	M	T	W	T	F	S	S
40				1	2	3	4
41	5	6	7	8	9	10	11
42	12	13	14	15	16	17	18
43	19	20	21	22	23	24	25
44	26	27	28	29	30	31	

October

26 Monday

Labour Day, holiday (NZ)

October Bank Holiday (R of I)

27 Tuesday

28 Wednesday

NAE SUCH LUCK, LADS . . .

HAW-HAW! WHIT DO YE LOOK LIKE?

IS IT NO' OBVIOUS? WE'RE GOIN' TAE PERFORM AS ABBA!

October / November

29 Thursday

---

30 Friday

---

31 Saturday

Halloween

---

1 Sunday

All Saints' Day

Canadian Daylight Saving Time ends (most locations)

Wk	M	T	W	T	F	S	S
40				1	2	3	4
41	5	6	7	8	9	10	11
42	12	13	14	15	16	17	18
43	19	20	21	22	23	24	25
44	26	27	28	29	30	31	

November

Those twins are always findin' somethin' tae laugh aboot, the blighters. So I couldnae believe it when they ran up tae me the other day lookin' a' serious.

'Horace! Horace! Whit's a' them explosions in the sky? And a' that rackit? Whit's goin' on?' they wailed in unison.

When I realised whit they were on aboot, I laughed tae mysel.

'Ha! The fireworks? Ye mean the fireworks?'

Weel. I already knew the poem inside oot. Besides, I needed tae educate these lads.

'Come sit doon, and I'll tell ye the story o' Guy Fawkes.'

THE FIFTH OF NOVEMBER
Remember, remember the fifth of November
Gunpowder, treason and plot.
We see no reason, why gunpowder
treason
Should ever be forgot.

Guy Fawkes, guy, t'was his intent
To blow up king and parliament.
Three score barrels were laid below
To prove old England's overthrow.

But by God's mercy he was catch'd
With a darkened lantern and burning match.
So, holler boys, holler boys, Let the bells ring.
Holler boys, holler boys, God save the king.

I finished the last verse – with a majestic delivery, if I do say so mysel' – and the twins were lookin' up at me, eyes wide, in deid silence. 'Finally,' I thought. 'I knew I could make 'em listen eventually.'

'Weel?' I said.

Suddenly – tae mah dismay – they exploded wi' laughter.

'Whit?' I yelled. 'Whit's so funny?!'

'Mr Fawkes must have been daft. We never get caught and we're always uptae trouble!'

November

2 Monday

All Souls' Day

Holiday (NZ: Marlborough)

Recreation Day, holiday (Aus: Northern Aus)

3 Tuesday

Melbourne Cup, holiday (Aus: VIC)

4 Wednesday

November

5 Thursday

Guy Fawkes Night (UK)

6 Friday

7 Saturday

8 Sunday

Remembrance Sunday

Wk	M	T	W	T	F	S	S
44							1
45	2	3	4	5	6	7	8
46	9	10	11	12	13	14	15
47	16	17	18	19	20	21	22
48	23	24	25	26	27	28	29
49	30						

November

9 Monday

_____
_____
_____
_____
_____
_____
_____
_____
_____
_____
_____
_____
_____
_____
_____
_____
_____

10 Tuesday

_____
_____
_____
_____
_____
_____
_____
_____
_____
_____
_____
_____
_____
_____
_____
_____
_____

11 Wednesday

Remembrance Day

Bank Holiday (Can except ON, QC)

Veterans Day, holiday (US)

Diwali, Hindu festival of lights, begins

_____
_____
_____
_____
_____
_____
_____
_____
_____
_____
_____

November

12 Thursday

Muharram ends

13 Friday

Robert Louis Stevenson Day

Holiday (NZ: Canterbury)

14 Saturday

15 Sunday

Diwali ends

Wk	M	T	W	T	F	S	S
44							1
45	2	3	4	5	6	7	8
46	9	10	11	12	13	14	15
47	16	17	18	19	20	21	22
48	23	24	25	26	27	28	29
49	30						

November

16 Monday

17 Tuesday

18 Wednesday

November

19 Thursday

20 Friday

21 Saturday

22 Sunday

Wk	M	T	W	T	F	S	S
44							1
45	2	3	4	5	6	7	8
46	9	10	11	12	13	14	15
47	16	17	18	19	20	21	22
48	23	24	25	26	27	28	29
49	30						

November

23 Monday

24 Tuesday

25 Wednesday

November

26 Thursday

Thanksgiving Day, holiday (US)

27 Friday

28 Saturday

29 Sunday

Advent Sunday

Wk	M	T	W	T	F	S	S
44							1
45	2	3	4	5	6	7	8
46	9	10	11	12	13	14	15
47	16	17	18	19	20	21	22
48	23	24	25	26	27	28	29
49	30						

December

Somebody once said that Christmas is a time for Faimily. Weel . . . whoever 'somebody' is, they clearly didnae have Faimily like this! Granpaw's asleep in front o' the telly already, Maw's fussin' over the turkey and lookin' like her heid's gonnae explode, and tae top it a' aff, the twins have swapped a' the jokes in the crackers for their own personal creations.

THE TWINS' CHRISTMAS CRACKERS

Q: Whit do you call ten bagpipes at the bottom of the sea?
A: A guid start!

Q: So, one year later – how's Granpaw's New Year's resolution holdin' up?
A: Grand. He's been walkin' five miles a day, so we cannae ever find him!

Q: Did you hear aboot Paw sellin' his best coat tae the charity shop? He's so generous, ain't he?
A: Generous?! He went and bought it back once they'd cleaned and pressed it!

THE BROONS

Scotland's Happy Family

November / December

30 Monday

Holiday (NZ: Chatham Islands, Westland)

1 Tuesday

2 Wednesday

December

3 Thursday

4 Friday

5 Saturday

6 Sunday

Wk	M	T	W	T	F	S	S
49		1	2	3	4	5	6
50	7	8	9	10	11	12	13
51	14	15	16	17	18	19	20
52	21	22	23	24	25	26	27
53	28	29	30	31			

December

7 Monday

Holiday (NZ: Chatham Islands, Westland)

8 Tuesday

9 Wednesday

December

10 Thursday

Human Rights Day

11 Friday

Anniversary of the Statute of Westminister (Can)

12 Saturday

13 Sunday

Wk	M	T	W	T	F	S	S
49		1	2	3	4	5	6
50	7	8	9	10	11	12	13
51	14	15	16	17	18	19	20
52	21	22	23	24	25	26	27
53	28	29	30	31			

December

14 Monday
Hanukkah ends

15 Tuesday

16 Wednesday

December

17 Thursday

_____
_____
_____
_____
_____
_____
_____
_____
_____
_____
_____
_____
_____
_____
_____
_____
_____
_____
_____
_____
_____
_____
_____

18 Friday

_____
_____
_____
_____
_____
_____
_____
_____
_____
_____
_____
_____
_____
_____
_____
_____
_____
_____
_____
_____
_____
_____
_____

19 Saturday

_____
_____
_____
_____
_____
_____
_____
_____
_____

20 Sunday

_____
_____
_____
_____
_____
_____
_____
_____
_____

Wk	M	T	W	T	F	S	S
49		1	2	3	4	5	6
50	7	8	9	10	11	12	13
51	14	15	16	17	18	19	20
52	21	22	23	24	25	26	27
53	28	29	30	31			

December

21 Monday

22 Tuesday

Winter Solstice

23 Wednesday

December

24 Thursday

Christmas Eve

25 Friday

Christmas Day, holiday

26 Saturday

Boxing Day, holiday (except some areas of Can)

St Stephen's Day (R of I)

27 Sunday

Wk	M	T	W	T	F	S	S
49		1	2	3	4	5	6
50	7	8	9	10	11	12	13
51	14	15	16	17	18	19	20
52	21	22	23	24	25	26	27
53	28	29	30	31			

December

28 Monday

29 Tuesday

30 Wednesday

BRAW, EH ? YE CANNA BEAT A GUID NICHT WI' THE FAMILY A' TOGETHER!

December / January 2016

31 Thursday
Hogmanay (New Year's Eve)

1 Friday

2 Saturday

3 Sunday

Wk	M	T	W	T	F	S	S
49		1	2	3	4	5	6
50	7	8	9	10	11	12	13
51	14	15	16	17	18	19	20
52	21	22	23	24	25	26	27
53	28	29	30	31			

Auld Lang Syne

BURNS' ORIGINAL SCOTS VERSE

Should auld acquaintance be forgot,
and never brought to mind?
Should auld acquaintance be forgot,
and auld lang syne?

CHORUS:
For auld lang syne, my jo,
for auld land syne,
we'll tak a cup o' kindness yet,
for auld lang syne.

And surely ye'll be your pint-stowp!
and surely I'll be mine!
And we'll tak a cup o' kindness yet,
for auld lang syne.

CHORUS

We twa hae run about the braes,
and pou'd the gowan fine;
but we've wander'd mony a weary fitt,
sin' auld lang syne.

CHORUS

We twa hae paidl'd in the burn,
frae morning sun till dine;
but seas between us braid hae roar'd
sin auld lang syne.

CHORUS

And there's a hand, my trusty fiere!
And gie's a hand o' thine!
And we'll tak a right gude-willie waught,
for auld lang syne.

CHORUS

ENGLISH TRANSLATION

Should old acquaintance be forgot,
and never brought to mind?
Should old acquaintance be forgot,
and old lang syne?

CHORUS:
For auld lang syne, my dear,
for auld lang syne,
we'll take a cup of kindness yet,
for auld lang syne.

And surely you'll buy your pint cup!
And surely I'll buy mine!
And we'll take a cup of kindness yet,
for old lang syne.

CHORUS

We two have run about the slopes,
and picked the daisies fine;
but we've wandered many a weary foot,
since old lang syne.

CHORUS

We two have paddled in the stream,
from morning sun till dine;
but seas between us broad have roared
since old lang syne.

CHORUS

And here's a hand, my trusty
friend!
And give me a hand of thine!
And we'll take a right good-will
draught,
for old land syne.

CHORUS

Maw's Hogmanay Steak Pie

This delicious pie is perfect for Hogmanay night or Ne'er Day wi' the first footers tae tuck intae. It's better tae mak' this the nicht afore ye want tae eat, tae mak' sure a' the meat is tender and fallin' apart.

You Will Need

A medium-sized pie dish
Tin foil

Ingredients

6 rump steaks
1 onion
2 glasses red wine
1 litre beef stock
2 egg yolks
500g puff pastry
Salt and pepper to season

Method

1. Heat oven tae 120ºC/Gas 1/2 and warm the pie dish.

2. Cut rump steaks intae cubes and season wi' salt and pepper.

3. Heat oil in a pan and quickly broon the steak cubes in batches, placin' them in the pie dish once brooned. They dinnae need tae be cooked yet, jist sealed.

4. Chop onion intae small pieces and mix wi' steak in the pie dish.

5. Add the wine intae the pot ye brooned the steak in and reduce by half, scraping a' the steak bits and juices from the bottom o' the pot. Add beef stock tae the wine, mix and heat through.

6. Add the stock and wine to the beef in the pie dish, cover tightly wi' foil and place in the oven for 2 hours, checkin' and stirrin' occasionally. Allow tae cool, then refrigerate overnight tae let the meat soak in the juices from the gravy.

7. The next morning, heat oven tae 200ºC/Gas 6. Remove foil frae pie dish and place in oven for 30 minutes. Add more stock if gravy is too thick or cornflour mixed first wi' cold watter if ye want it thicker.

8. Roll oot the puff pastry and cover the pie dish, brush wi' a wee bit o' egg yolk. Put a wee hole in the middle o' the pastry, tae allow the steam tae escape.

9. Return tae oven and cook for a further 20 minutes or until pastry is as broon as ye like it. Then serve up tae the hungry family.

Famous Scots

Here are a few famous Scottish folk ye should ken.

Billy Connolly
24 November 1942 – present, born in Glasgow

Also known in Scotland as 'The Big Yin' ('The Big One'), Connolly is a comedian, musician, actor and presenter. Though he originally started out as a welder in the Glasgow shipyards, he gave it up to become a folk singer and banjo player in The Humblebums in the early 1960s. In the early 1970s, he developed his humorous folk singing career into full-fledged comedy.

Andy Murray
15 May 1987 – present, born in Dunblane

Ranked at World no. 9 professional tennis player and British no. 1 since February 2006, Andy Murray has had a successful tennis career that many Scots are proud of. Andy won his first tournament as an under-10 junior at the Dunblane Sports Club, where it became apparent that we was destined for success.

Robert Burns
25 January 1759 – 21 July 1796, born in Ayrshire

Robert Burns was a Scottish poet and lyricist and is widely regarded as the national poet of Scotland and is celebrated worldwide. His poem and song 'Auld Lang Syne' is often sung at Hogmanany (New Year's Eve) across the world, in Scots and in English.

Alex Salmond
31 December 1954 – present, born in Linlithgow

In May 2007, Salmond became the fourth First Minister of Scotland and concurrently he was the leader of the Scottish National Party (SNP). Salmond was one of the foremost proponents of the Scottish Independence Referendum, which the people of Scotland placed their votes for on 18 September 2014.

James Watt
30 January 1736 – 25 August 1819, born in Greenock

Fundamental to the changes brought by the Industrial Revolution, Scottish inventor and mechanical engineer James Watt made enhancements to the Newcomen steam engine. Watt, the unit of power, is named after him.

Sir Walter Scott
15 August 1771 – 21 September 1832, born in Edinburgh

A Scottish historical novelist, playwright and poet, Scott was the first English-language author to have had international success in his lifetime. His style of writing, which involved extensive pages of stream of consciousness, gives readers insights into the politics and agriculture of Scott's time.

Susan Boyle
1 April 1961 – present, born in Blackburn

Starting as a contestant on the TV programme *Britain's Got Talent*, Susan is now a household name and her debut album became the number one best-selling album in 2009. Nearly everyone has heard her cover of 'I Dreamed a Dream' from *Les Misérables*.

William Wallace
c.1270 – 23 August 1305, born in Renfrewshire

A Scottish landowner who became one of the main leaders during the Wars of Scottish Independence. Sir William Wallace famously defeated an English army at the Battle of Stirling Bridge in 1297. In 1305, Wallace was captured and was hanged, drawn and quartered for high treason and crimes against English civilians. Wallace has become an iconic figure in Scotland's past and its national identity.

Sean Connery
25 August 1930 – present, born in Edinburgh

Best known for portraying the character 'James Bond', Sir Sean is an actor and producer who has won an Academy Award, two BAFTA and three Golden Globes. He was knighted by Queen Elizabeth II in 2000.

Mary, Queen of Scots
8 December 1542 – 8 February 1587, born in Linlithgow

The only surviving legitimate child of King James V of Scotland, Mary Stuart was only six days old when she acceded to the throne. She spent most of her childhood in France while Scotland was ruled by regents. Her complicated personal life and political ignorance eventually led to her being imprisoned and executed by Elizabeth I.

Sir Arthur Conan Doyle
22 May 1859 – 7 July 1930, born in Edinburgh

A Scottish physician and writer, who is most famous for his fictional stories about the detective *Sherlock Holmes*, which are considered as milestones in crime fiction writing. He also popularised the mystery of the abandoned ship *Mary Celeste* and his other works included fantasy, plays, poetry and historical novels.

Greyfriars Bobby
c. 1855 or 1856 – 14 January 1872

A dog who became famous in the nineteenth-century for supposedly spending fourteen years guarding the grave of his owner, John Gray, until he died himself. His story continues to be active as oral history in Edinburgh and through books, films and stories. There is a commemorative statue of Bobby near Greyfriars Kirkyard in Edinburgh.

Scots Words and Sayings

'To put someone's gas at a peep'
To destroy someone's enthusiasm by
putting them in their place.

'Do ye ken likesay Joe Smith?'
Are you acquainted with Joe Smith?

'I'm fair puggled.' I'm short of breath.

'Haud yer wheesht!' Be quiet.

'Dinnae fash yersel!' Don't worry.

'Fu' the noo.' Full for now (after a meal).

'All his eggs are double-yoakit.'
Refers to someone who boasts/speaks
very highly of themselves.

'He's no' the fu' shillin'.'
Refers to someone who isn't particularly smart.

'You're the wee hen that never layed away.'
Refers to someone who is feigning innocence.

'Ye'll have had yer tea.'
A notorious Scottish welcome into a home.

Scots Sayings Continued

'Into everything but a working jaiket.' Refers to
someone who is workshy/unemployed.

'Lying there like a ludgin' hoose cat.'
Refers to somebody lazing around.

'Tatties over the side.'
Everything is going/has gone wrong at once.

'Put your feet oan.' Go for a walk.

'He gie's me the Jaundice.'
He is disgusting.

'Corrie jouket.' Left handed.

'It's a lang road that's no goat a turnin'.'
Things have to change eventually.

'Black affronted.'
Very embarrassed and/or humiliated.

'A coo's lick.' A quick wipe of
the face with a damp cloth.

'Sling a dinghy.' To ignore someone.

'Have a shuftie.' To have a small peek.

'Awa an' bile yer heid an'
make daft soup.' Get lost.

'Ye'll dee a thoosand deaths ye'll never dee.'
You'll die a thousand deaths you'll never die –
i.e. you worry too much.

'Yer faither wisnae a glazier.'
You are blocking my view (usually of the TV).

'Ma heid was gi'en me gip.'
My head was really sore.

'Ah could eat a dug wi' the mange.'
I'm very hungry.

'Yer jaiket's oan a shoogly peg.' You're in trouble.

'The Leith police dismisseth us.'
An old Edinburgh tongue-twister.

Baffies – slippers
Bairn – child
Baltic – freezing cold
Bevvy – alcoholic drink
Boggin' – filthy/disgusting
Bonnie – beautiful
Bowfin' – smelly
Breeks – trousers
Brither – brother
Bummle – sing badly
Bunker – kitcken worktop surface
But an' ben – a two-roomed house
Cauld cutes – cold feet
Chappin' – knocking
Chitterin' – shivering
Clour – a swelling that follows a blow
Clype – to tell tales on someone
Coo – cow
Crabbit - grumpy
Craw – to boast
Daft days – days between Christmas and New Year
Daunder – a stroll
Dicht or dight – to wipe
Donnybrucker – fist fight
Dour – glum
Dreich – cold, damp, miserable weather
Drookit – drenched
Drouthy – thirsty
Dunt – a hit or a blow
Fitba – football
Fly – cunning/devious

Footer – to fidget
Geggie – mouth
Glaikit – stupid
Glegness – cleverness
Gowf – golf
Gowpin – painful, throbbing
Hoachin' – a very busy crowd
Ill-trickit – mischievous
Ken – know
Langsome – slow and tedious
Lugs – ears
Lum – chimney
Manky – disgusting
Messages – groceries
Muckle – big
Numpty – an idiot
Peely Wally – pale
Piece – a sandwich
Plank – to hide something
Pliskie – a prank or a joke
Queyn or quine – a girl
Scran – food
Scud – a blow
Scunnered – exasperated
Shunky – toilet
Skelp – slap
Sleekit – cunning/sly
Sonsie – jolly
Squibs – fireworks
Stoatin – bounce about/ wander
Swally – to drink
Tapsalteerie – upside down
Tattie – potato
Tattyboggler – scarecrow
Wee – small
Wheech – whoosh

The Dashing White Sergeant

A ceilidh widnae be a ceilidh without the Dashing White Sergeant. The Dashing White Sergeant has been a favourite since the nineteenth century and the title comes frae even before that: it's from an eighteenth-century song aboot a lassie who wants tae dress up as a soldier tae follow her sweetheart oot ontae the battlefields. But dinnae worry, there'll be nae battles here – unless it's the lassies fightin' tae be your partner! And for this dance ye need twa partners: either one man and twa women, or one woman and twa men.

Formation: Three facing three in a circle around the room.
Music: 'The Dashing White Sergeant'.
Bars: 32

Bars	Instructions
1-8	In your line of three, join hands wi' the three standin' in front of you and all circle to the left for eight steps and then back to the right for eight steps.
9-12	Release hands, and in your threes, the partner in the middle turns to the partner on their right and does a pas de basque, then uses their right hand to turn them. (The third partner stands still while this is happening.)
13-16	Repeat the above with the other dancer.
17-24	Using an elbow grip, the middle partner turns the right-hand partner, then the left-hand partner, then the right again, then the left again.
25-28	Then, back in your line of three and holding hands, advance towards the opposite three and retire.
29-32	Finally, both lines dance forward, with one line raising their hands tae mak' an archway so the other line can dance underneath. Meet wi' the next line o' three and start all over again!

Star-signs

Aries. The Ram
March 21st – April 19th
Personality: Determined, fiery, born leader, impulsive, opinionated and ambitious.
Lucky days: Mondays, Tuesdays, Thursdays and Sundays.
Mantra: I am the best, yet I am humble.

Taurus. The Bull
April 20th – May 20th
Personality: Resolute, dependable, secure, proud, decisive and faithful.
Lucky days: Wednesdays, Fridays and Saturdays.
Mantra: I am secure and without need.

Gemini. The Twins
May 21st – June 20th
Personality: Multi-talented, thinker, talkative, social, diverse interests and loves variety.
Lucky days: Wednesdays, Fridays and Saturdays.
Mantra: I am calm.

Cancer. The Crab
June 21st – July 22nd
Personality: Loving, sensual, faithful, instinctive, moody and charitable.
Lucky days: Mondays, Tuesdays and Thursdays.
Mantra: I am lovable as well as loving.

Leo. The Lion
July 23rd – August 22nd
Personality: Original, majestic, charitable, ambitious, loyal and physical.
Lucky days: Sundays, Mondays, Tuesdays and Thursdays.
Mantra: I am calm and satisfied.

Virgo. The Maiden
August 23rd – September 22nd
Personality: Loving, susceptible, sympathetic, sensual, faithful and instinctive.
Lucky days: Wednesdays, Fridays and Saturdays.
Mantra: I am relaxed and deserve to be served as well as serve.

Libra. The Scales
September 23rd – October 22nd
Personality: Refined, social, artistic, intellectual, communicative and concerned with relationships.
Lucky days: Wednesdays, Fridays and Saturdays.
Mantra: I am harmonious in body, mind and spirit

Scorpio. The Scorpion
October 23rd – November 21st
Personality: Secretive, resolute, insensitive, painstaking, stubborn and passionate.
Lucky days: Mondays, Tuesdays, Thursdays and Sundays.
Mantra: I don't need to control everything. I am free and peaceful.

Sagittarius. The Archer
November 22nd – December 21st
Personality: Magnanimous, honest, generous, reckless, proud and free.
Lucky days: Tuesdays, Thursdays, Fridays, Saturdays and Sundays.
Mantra: I am generous and loving to myself as well as to others.

Capricorn. The Goat
December 22nd – January 19th
Personality: Loving, sympathetic, charitable, instinctive, over-reactive and moody.
Lucky days: Wednesday, Fridays and Saturdays.
Mantra: I am successful and content.

Aquarius. The Water Bearer
January 20th – February 18th
Personality: Humane, progressive, intellectual, sympathetic, flamboyant and unpredictable.
Lucky days: Wednesdays, Fridays and Saturdays.
Mantra: I evolve and encompass all humanity.

Pisces. The Fish
February 19th – March 20th
Personality: Loving, sensitive, intuitive, spiritual, idealistic and moody.
Lucky days: Mondays, Tuesdays, Thursdays and Sundays.
Mantra: I offer my love to all, but I am grounded.

Picture credits:

All illustrations are credited to The Broons®
© DC Thomson & Co. Ltd. 2014
Famous Scots and Star Signs images:
Shutterstock.com
(Arthur Conan Doyle: PA Images)

First published 2014
by Black & White Publishing Ltd
29 Ocean Drive, Edinburgh EH6 6JL

1 3 5 7 9 10 8 6 4 2   14 15 16 17

ISBN: 978 1 910230 09 1

Text copyright © Black & White Publishing Ltd, 2014 and DC Thomson & Co. Ltd. 2014
The Broons logo and supporting characters (excluding elements listed in picture credits)
appear courtesy of, and are copyright The Broons ®© DC Thomson & Co. Ltd. 2014

www.thebroons.com

All rights reserved. No part of this publication may be reproduced, stored in a
retrieval system, or transmitted in any form, or by any means, electronic, mechanical,
photocopying, recording or otherwise, without permission in writing from the publisher.

A CIP catalogue record for this book is available from the British Library.

Typeset by Creative Link, North Berwick
Printed and bound in Poland by www.hussarbooks.pl

2016

JANUARY

S	M	T	W	T	F	S
					1	2
3	4	5	6	7	8	9
10	11	12	13	14	15	16
17	18	19	20	21	22	23
24	25	26	27	28	29	30
31						

FEBRUARY

S	M	T	W	T	F	S
	1	2	3	4	5	6
7	8	9	10	11	12	13
14	15	16	17	18	19	20
21	22	23	24	25	26	27
28	29					

MARCH

S	M	T	W	T	F	S
		1	2	3	4	5
6	7	8	9	10	11	12
13	14	15	16	17	18	19
20	21	22	23	24	25	26
27	28	29	30	31		

APRIL

S	M	T	W	T	F	S
					1	2
3	4	5	6	7	8	9
10	11	12	13	14	15	16
17	18	19	20	21	22	23
24	25	26	27	28	29	30

MAY

S	M	T	W	T	F	S
1	2	3	4	5	6	7
8	9	10	11	12	13	14
15	16	17	18	19	20	21
22	23	24	25	26	27	28
29	30	31				

JUNE

S	M	T	W	T	F	S
			1	2	3	4
5	6	7	8	9	10	11
12	13	14	15	16	17	18
19	20	21	22	23	24	25
26	27	28	29	30		

JULY

S	M	T	W	T	F	S
					1	2
3	4	5	6	7	8	9
10	11	12	13	14	15	16
17	18	19	20	21	22	23
24	25	26	27	28	29	30
31						

AUGUST

S	M	T	W	T	F	S
	1	2	3	4	5	6
7	8	9	10	11	12	13
14	15	16	17	18	19	20
21	22	23	24	25	26	27
28	29	30	31			

SEPTEMBER

S	M	T	W	T	F	S
				1	2	3
4	5	6	7	8	9	10
11	12	13	14	15	16	17
18	19	20	21	22	23	24
25	26	27	28	29	30	

OCTOBER

S	M	T	W	T	F	S
						1
2	3	4	5	6	7	8
9	10	11	12	13	14	15
16	17	18	19	20	21	22
23	24	25	26	27	28	29
30	31					

NOVEMBER

S	M	T	W	T	F	S
		1	2	3	4	5
6	7	8	9	10	11	12
13	14	15	16	17	18	19
20	21	22	23	24	25	26
27	28	29	30			

DECEMBER

S	M	T	W	T	F	S
				1	2	3
4	5	6	7	8	9	10
11	12	13	14	15	16	17
18	19	20	21	22	23	24
25	26	27	28	29	30	31